Printed in the USA
CPSIA information can be obtained
at www.ICGtesting.com
JSHW052014140824
68134JS00006B/109

9 781683 362913

About The Art of Jewish Living Series by Dr. Ron Wolfson

The Art of Jewish Living, a project of the Federation of Jewish Men's Clubs and American Jewish University, is a series of books designed for adults and families seeking to enter the center of Jewish life. Each volume features real Jewish families reflecting on their experiences with Jewish practice, along with detailed information and instruction on the performance and meaning of Jewish celebration.

OTHER GUIDES IN THE ART OF JEWISH LIVING SERIES

Hanukkah, 2nd Edition

The Family Guide to Spiritual Celebration

Hands-on advice and practical suggestions for every aspect of family celebration.

7 x 9, 240 pp, Illus., Quality Paperback Original
ISBN 978-1-58023-122-0

Shabbat, 2nd Edition

The Family Guide to Preparing for and Celebrating the Sabbath

Information about every aspect of the holy day, and all the resources needed to prepare for and celebrate it.

7 x 9, 320 pp, Illus., Quality Paperback Original
ISBN 978-1-58023-164-0

Also available are these helpful companions to *Shabbat:*

- Audiocassette of the Blessings, DN03
- Booklet of Blessings and Songs, ISBN 978-1-879045-91-0
- Teacher's Guide, ISBN 978-1-879045-92-7

Passover, 2nd Edition

The Family Guide to Spiritual Celebration

Explains concepts, ritual, and ceremony with step-by-step procedures for observance.

7 x 9, 416 pp, Quality Paperback Original
ISBN 978-1-58023-174-9

Also available are these helpful companions to *Passover:*

- Passover Workbook, ISBN 978-1-879045-94-1
- Audiocassette of the Blessings and Songs, DN04

For more information about these and other Jewish Lights books, please visit our website at **www.jewishlights.com.**

1

הֲכָנָה לְשַׁבָּת *HAKHANAH L'SHABBAT*
PREPARATION FOR SHABBAT

A festive Shabbat celebration requires preparation: preparing the home, preparing the meal, preparing the self. In honor of Shabbat, we contribute *tzedakah* for the support of the Jewish community.

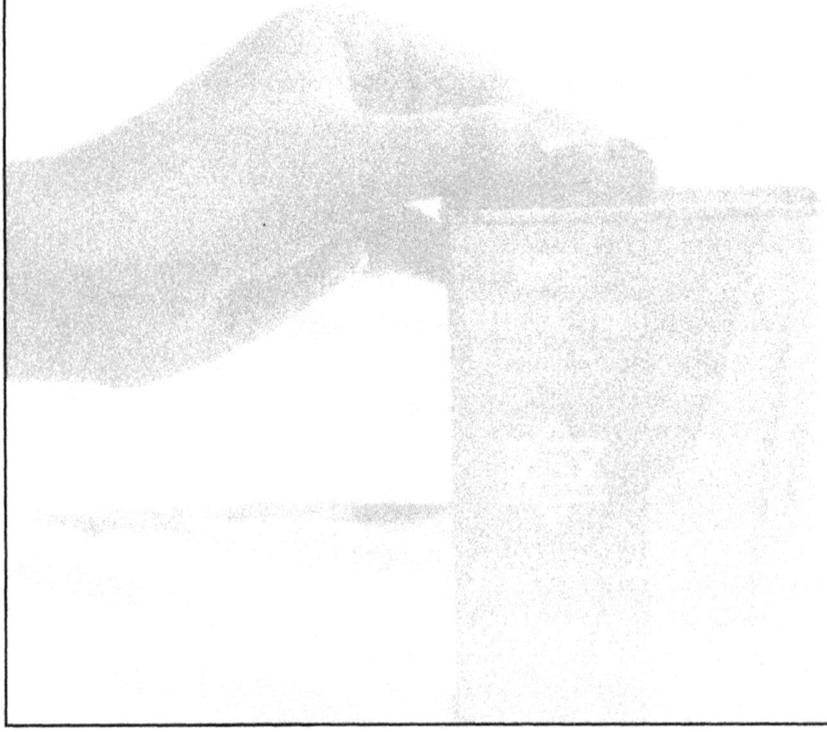

2

הַדְלָקַת נֵרוֹת *HADLAKAT NEROT*
CANDLE LIGHTING

At least two candles are lit, the eyes covered and the blessing recited. Upon completing the blessing, look at the lights and wish each other "Shabbat Shalom."

בָּרוּךְ אַתָּה יְיָ,	*Barukh attah Adonai*
אֱלֹהֵינוּ מֶלֶךְ הָעוֹלָם,	*Eloheinu melekh ha-olam*
אֲשֶׁר קִדְּשָׁנוּ בְּמִצְוֹתָיו	*asher kidshanu b'mitzvotav*
וְצִוָּנוּ לְהַדְלִיק נֵר שֶׁל	*v'tzivanu l'hadlik ner shel*
שַׁבָּת.	*Shabbat.*

Praised are You, Adonai,
our God, Ruler of the Universe,
who made us holy through the commandments
and commanded us to kindle the Shabbat lights.

3

שָׁלוֹם עֲלֵיכֶם *SHALOM ALEIKHEM*

PEACE BE TO YOU

As we gather at the table, we join in singing this traditional hymn welcoming the Shabbat:

שָׁלוֹם עֲלֵיכֶם מַלְאֲכֵי	*Shalom aleikhem malakhei*
הַשָּׁרֵת	*ha-shareit*
מַלְאֲכֵי עֶלְיוֹן,	*malakhei Elyon*
מִמֶּלֶךְ מַלְכֵי הַמְּלָכִים	*mimelekh malkhei ha-melakhim*
הַקָּדוֹשׁ בָּרוּךְ הוּא.	*ha-Kadosh barukh hu.*

Peace be to you ministering angels, angels of the Most High
from the Ruler, the Ruler of Rulers, The Holy One, the One to be praised.

בּוֹאֲכֶם לְשָׁלוֹם מַלְאֲכֵי	*Bo'akhem l'shalom malakhei*
הַשָּׁלוֹם	*ha-shalom*
מַלְאֲכֵי עֶלְיוֹן,	*malakhei Elyon*
מִמֶּלֶךְ מַלְכֵי הַמְּלָכִים	*mimelekh malkhei ha-melakhim*
הַקָּדוֹשׁ בָּרוּךְ הוּא.	*ha-Kadosh barukh hu.*

Come in peace, angels of peace, angels of the Most High
from the Ruler, the Ruler of Rulers, The Holy One, the One to be praised.

בָּרְכוּנִי לְשָׁלוֹם מַלְאֲכֵי	*Barkhuni l'shalom malakhei*
הַשָּׁלוֹם	*ha-shalom*
מַלְאֲכֵי עֶלְיוֹן,	*malakhei Elyon*
מִמֶּלֶךְ מַלְכֵי הַמְּלָכִים	*mimelekh malkhei ha-melakhim*
הַקָּדוֹשׁ בָּרוּךְ הוּא.	*ha-Kadosh barukh hu.*

Bless me with peace, angels of peace, angels of the Most High
from the Ruler, the Ruler of Rulers, The Holy One, the One to be praised.

צֵאתְכֶם לְשָׁלוֹם מַלְאֲכֵי	*Tzeitkhem l'shalom malakhei*
הַשָּׁלוֹם	*ha-shalom*
מַלְאֲכֵי עֶלְיוֹן,	*malakhei Elyon*
מִמֶּלֶךְ מַלְכֵי הַמְּלָכִים	*mimelekh malkhei ha-melakhim*
הַקָּדוֹשׁ בָּרוּךְ הוּא.	*ha-Kadosh barukh hu.*

Go in peace, angels of peace, angels of the Most High,
from the Ruler, the Ruler of Rulers, the Holy One, the One to be praised.

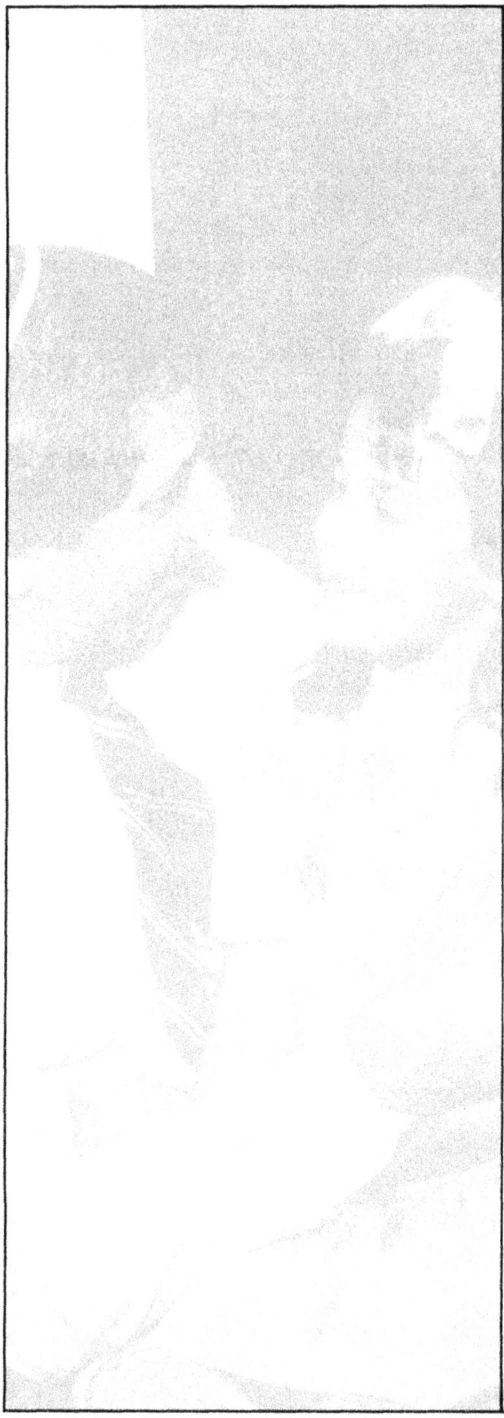

4

בִּרְכוֹת הַמִּשְׁפָּחָה

BIRKHOT HA-MISHPAḤAH

FAMILY BLESSINGS

יְשִׂימְךָ אֱלֹהִים
כְּאֶפְרַיִם וְכִמְנַשֶּׁה.

יְשִׂימֵךְ אֱלֹהִים
כְּשָׂרָה רִבְקָה רָחֵל וְלֵאָה.

יְבָרֶכְךָ יְיָ
וְיִשְׁמְרֶךָ,
יָאֵר יְיָ פָּנָיו אֵלֶיךָ
וִיחֻנֶּךָּ,
יִשָּׂא יְיָ פָּנָיו אֵלֶיךָ
וְיָשֵׂם לְךָ שָׁלוֹם.

In the spirit of *sh'lom bayit*—"peace in the home"—we offer blessings for our children.

For the Sons

Y'simkha Elohim

k'Efrayim v'khiMenashe.

(May) God make you like Ephraim and Menasseh.

For the Daughters

Y'simeikh Elohim

k'Sarah Rivka Raḥel v'Leah.

(May) God make you like Sarah, Rebecca, Rachel, and Leah.

For all Children

Y'varekh'kha Adonai

v'yishm'rekha.

Ya'er Adonai panav elekha

viḥuneka.

Yisa Adonai panav elekha

v'yasem l'kha shalom.

(May) the Lord bless you and watch over you.
(May) the Lord cause the Divine face to shine upon you and be gracious to you.
(May) the Lord lift up the Divine face toward you and give you peace.

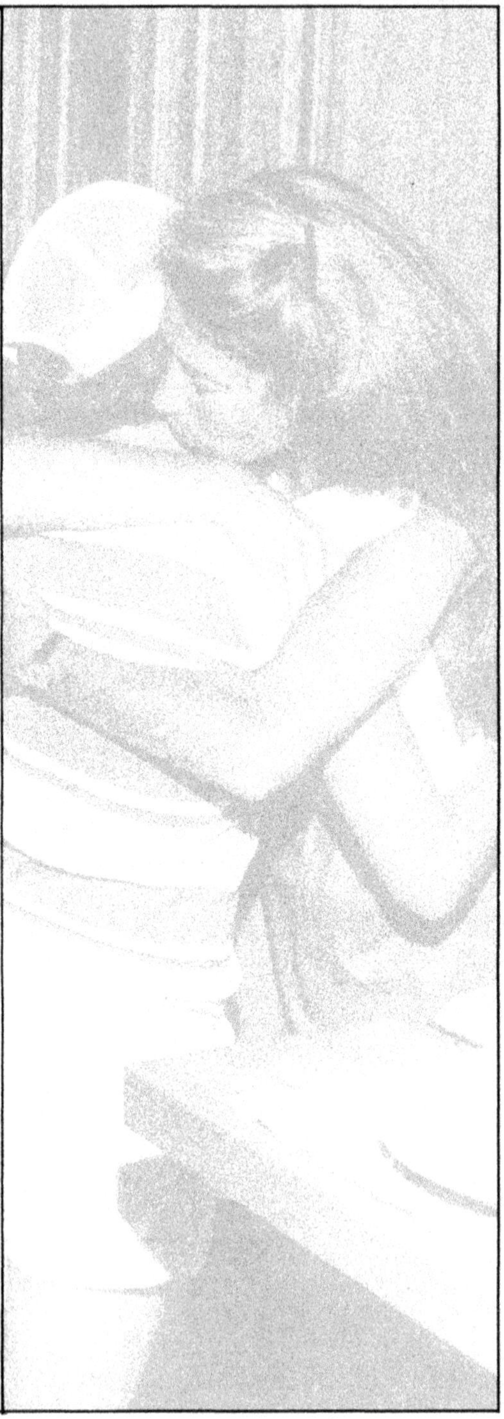

אֵשֶׁת חַיִל *EISHET ḤAYIL*

A Woman of Valor (Proverbs 31:10-31)

Turning to the parents, we offer words of praise.

אֵשֶׁת־חַיִל מִי יִמְצָא	*Eishet ḥayil mi yimtza*
וְרָחוֹק מִפְּנִינִים מִכְרָהּ:	*v'raḥok mip'ninim mikhrah.*
בָּטַח בָּהּ לֵב בַּעְלָהּ	*Bataḥ ba lev ba'lah*
וְשָׁלָל לֹא יֶחְסָר:	*v'shalal lo yeḥsar.*
גְּמָלַתְהוּ טוֹב וְלֹא־רָע	*G'malat'hu tov v'lo ra*
כֹּל יְמֵי חַיֶּיהָ:	*kol y'mei ḥayeha.*
דָּרְשָׁה צֶמֶר וּפִשְׁתִּים	*Darsha tzemer u-fishtim*
וַתַּעַשׂ בְּחֵפֶץ כַּפֶּיהָ:	*vata'as b'ḥefetz kape'ha.*
הָיְתָה כָּאֳנִיּוֹת סוֹחֵר	*Hay'ta ko'oniyot soḥer*
מִמֶּרְחָק תָּבִיא לַחְמָהּ:	*mimerḥak tavi laḥmah.*
וַתָּקָם בְּעוֹד לַיְלָה	*Vatakom b'od lilah*
וַתִּתֵּן טֶרֶף לְבֵיתָהּ	*vatiten teref l'veita*
וְחֹק לְנַעֲרֹתֶיהָ:	*v'ḥok l'na'aroteha.*
זָמְמָה שָׂדֶה וַתִּקָּחֵהוּ	*Zam'ma sadeh vatikaḥehu*
מִפְּרִי כַפֶּיהָ נָטְעָה כָּרֶם:	*mipri khape'ha nat'ah karem.*
חָגְרָה בְעוֹז מָתְנֶיהָ	*Ḥagrah v'oz motneha*
וַתְּאַמֵּץ זְרוֹעֹתֶיהָ:	*vat'ametz z'roteha.*
טָעֲמָה כִּי־טוֹב סַחְרָהּ	*Ta'amah ki tov saḥrah*
לֹא־יִכְבֶּה בַלַּיְלָה נֵרָהּ:	*lo yikhbeh valilah neirah.*
יָדֶיהָ שִׁלְּחָה בַכִּישׁוֹר	*Yadeha shilḥah vakishor*
וְכַפֶּיהָ תָּמְכוּ פָלֶךְ:	*v'khape'ha tamkhu falekh.*
כַּפָּהּ פָּרְשָׂה לֶעָנִי	*Kapah parsah le'ani*
וְיָדֶיהָ שִׁלְּחָה לָאֶבְיוֹן:	*v'yadeha shilḥah la'evyon.*
לֹא־תִירָא לְבֵיתָהּ מִשָּׁלֶג	*Lo tira l'veita mishaleg*
כִּי כָל־בֵּיתָהּ לָבֻשׁ שָׁנִים:	*ki khol beitah lavush shanim.*
מַרְבַדִּים עָשְׂתָה־לָּהּ	*Marvadim as'tah lah*
שֵׁשׁ וְאַרְגָּמָן לְבוּשָׁהּ:	*shesh v'argaman l'vushah.*
נוֹדָע בַּשְּׁעָרִים בַּעְלָהּ	*Noda ba'sh'arim ba'lah*
בְּשִׁבְתּוֹ עִם־זִקְנֵי אָרֶץ:	*b'shivto im ziknei aretz.*
סָדִין עָשְׂתָה וַתִּמְכֹּר	*Sadin as'tah vatimkor*
וַחֲגוֹר נָתְנָה לַכְּנַעֲנִי:	*vaḥagor natnah lak'na'ni.*

עֹז־וְהָדָר לְבוּשָׁהּ	*Oz v'hadar l'vushah*
וַתִּשְׂחַק לְיוֹם אַחֲרוֹן:	*vatisḥak l'yom aḥaron.*
פִּיהָ פָּתְחָה בְחָכְמָה	*Pi'ha pat'ḥah v'ḥokhmah*
וְתוֹרַת־חֶסֶד עַל־לְשׁוֹנָהּ:	*v'torat ḥesed al l'shonah.*
צוֹפִיָּה הֲלִיכוֹת בֵּיתָהּ	*Tzofi'a halikhot beitah*
וְלֶחֶם עַצְלוּת לֹא תֹאכֵל:	*v'leḥem atzlut lo tokhel.*
קָמוּ בָנֶיהָ וַיְאַשְּׁרוּהָ	*Kamu vaneha vayashruha*
בַּעְלָהּ וַיְהַלְלָהּ:	*ba'lah va'y'hal'lah.*
רַבּוֹת בָּנוֹת עָשׂוּ חָיִל	*Rabot banot asu ḥayil*
וְאַתְּ עָלִית עַל־כֻּלָּנָה:	*v'at alit al kulanah.*
שֶׁקֶר הַחֵן וְהֶבֶל הַיֹּפִי	*Sheker ha-ḥen v'hevel ha-yofi*
אִשָּׁה יִרְאַת־יְיָ הִיא תִתְהַלָּל:	*isha yirat Adonai hi tit'halal.*
תְּנוּ־לָהּ מִפְּרִי יָדֶיהָ	*T'nu la mipri yadeha*
וִיהַלְלוּהָ בַשְּׁעָרִים מַעֲשֶׂיהָ:	*viyhal'luha vash'arim ma'aseha.*

A good wife, who can find?
She is more precious than corals.
The heart of her husband trusts in her,
And he has no lack of gain.
She does him good and not harm
All the days of her life.
She seeks out wool and flax
And works it up as her hands will.
She is like the ships of the merchant,
From afar she brings her food.
She arises while it is yet night,
And gives food to her household,
And a portion to her maidens.
She examines a field and buys it,
With the fruit of her hands she plants a vineyard.
She girds herself with strength,
And braces her arms for work.
She perceives that her profit is good;
Her lamp does not go out at night.
She lays her hands on the distaff,
Her palms grasp the spindle.
She opens her hand to the poor,
And extends her hands to the needy.
She does not fear snow for her household,
For all her household are clad in warm garments.
Coverlets she makes for herself;
Her clothing is fine linen and purple.
Her husband is distinguished in the council
When he sits among the elders of the land.
She makes linen cloth and sells it,
She delivers belts to the merchant.
Strength and honor are her garb,
She smiles confidently at the future.
She opens her mouth with wisdom,
And the teaching of kindness is on her tongue.
She looks well to the ways of her household,
She eats not the bread of idleness.
Her children rise up and call her blessed,
And her husband praises her:
"Many daughters have done excellently,
But you excel them all."
Grace is deceptive and beauty is passing;
A woman revering Adonai, she shall be praised.
Give her of the fruit of her hands,
And let her own works praise her in the gates.

אַשְׁרֵי־אִישׁ *ASHREI ISH*

Happy is the Man (Psalm 112)

הַלְלוּ־יָהּ	*Hal'luyah.*
אַשְׁרֵי־אִישׁ יָרֵא אֶת־יְיָ	*Ashrei ish yarei et Adonai*
בְּמִצְוֺתָיו חָפֵץ מְאֹד׃	*b'mitzvotav ḥafetz m'od.*
גִּבּוֹר בָּאָרֶץ יִהְיֶה זַרְעוֹ	*Gibor ba'aretz yiyeh zaro*
דּוֹר יְשָׁרִים יְבֹרָךְ׃	*dor y'sharim y'vorakh.*
הוֹן־וָעֹשֶׁר בְּבֵיתוֹ	*Hon va'osher b'veito*
וְצִדְקָתוֹ עֹמֶדֶת לָעַד׃	*v'tzid'kato omedet la'ad.*
זָרַח בַּחֹשֶׁךְ אוֹר	*Zaraḥ ba'ḥoshekh or*
לַיְשָׁרִים.	*la-y'sharim*
חַנּוּן וְרַחוּם וְצַדִּיק׃	*Ḥanun v'raḥum v'tzadik....*
מִשְּׁמוּעָה רָעָה לֹא יִירָא	*Mish'mu'ah ra'ah lo yira*
נָכוֹן לִבּוֹ בָּטֻחַ	*Nakhon libo batu'aḥ*
בַּייָ׃	*ba'Adonai.*
סָמוּךְ לִבּוֹ לֹא יִירָא	*Samukh libo lo yira....*
פִּזַּר נָתַן לָאֶבְיוֹנִים	*Pizar natan la'evyonim*
צִדְקָתוֹ עֹמֶדֶת לָעַד	*tzidkato omedet la'ad.*
קַרְנוֹ תָּרוּם בְּכָבוֹד׃	*Karno tarum b'khavod.....*

Halleluya!
Happy is the man who reveres Adonai,
Who greatly delights in God's commandments.
His descendants will be honored in the land,
The generation of the upright will be praised.
His household prospers
And his righteousness endures forever.
Light dawns in the darkness for the upright;
For the one who is gracious, compassionate and just....
He is not afraid of evil tidings;
His mind is firm, trusting in Adonai.
His heart is steady, he will not be afraid....
He has given to the poor.
His righteousness endures forever,
His life is exalted in honor ...

בִּרְכַּת הַמִּשְׁפָּחָה *BIRKAT HA-MISHPAḤAH*
Family Blessing

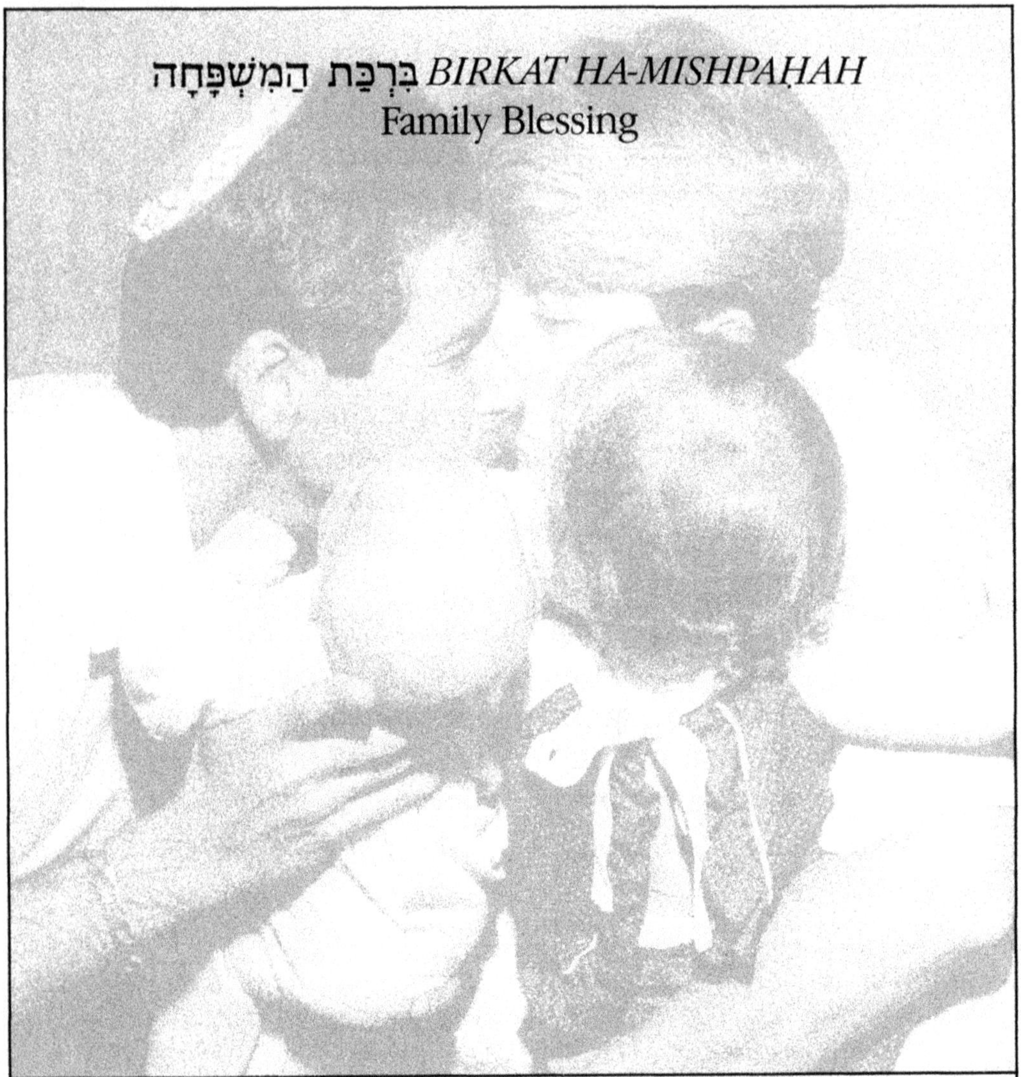

הָרַחֲמָן	*Ha-Raḥaman*
הוּא יְבָרֵךְ	*hu y'vareikh*
אוֹתָנוּ כֻּלָּנוּ יַחַד	*otanu kulanu yaḥad*
בְּבִרְכַּת שָׁלוֹם	*b'virkat shalom.*

May the Merciful One bless all of us together with the blessing of peace.

5

קִדּוּשׁ *KIDDUSH*
SANCTIFICATION OF THE DAY

By reciting the *Kiddush*, we acknowledge the sanctity of the Shabbat through blessing a cup of wine. The cup is lifted and we say:

Vayekhulu

וַיְהִי עֶרֶב וַיְהִי בֹקֶר	*Vay'hi erev vay'hi voker:*
יוֹם הַשִּׁשִּׁי.	*yom ha-shishi.*
וַיְכֻלּוּ הַשָּׁמַיִם	*Vayekhulu ha-shamayim*
וְהָאָרֶץ וְכָל־צְבָאָם.	*V'ha-aretz v'khol tz'va'am.*
וַיְכַל אֱלֹהִים בַּיּוֹם	*Vay'khal Elohim bayom*
הַשְּׁבִיעִי	*ha-shvi'i*
מְלַאכְתּוֹ אֲשֶׁר עָשָׂה,	*m'lakhto asher asa;*
וַיִּשְׁבֹּת בַּיּוֹם הַשְּׁבִיעִי	*Va'yishbot bayom ha-shvi'i*
מִכָּל־מְלַאכְתּוֹ אֲשֶׁר עָשָׂה.	*mikol m'lakhto asher asa.*
וַיְבָרֶךְ אֱלֹהִים אֶת־יוֹם	*Vay'varekh Elohim et yom*
הַשְּׁבִיעִי,	*ha-shvi'i*
וַיְקַדֵּשׁ אוֹתוֹ,	*vay'kadesh oto*
כִּי בוֹ שָׁבַת מִכָּל־	*ki vo shavat mikol*
מְלַאכְתּוֹ	*m'lakhto*
אֲשֶׁר בָּרָא אֱלֹהִים לַעֲשׂוֹת.	*asher bara Elohim la'asot.*

And there was evening and there was morning: the sixth day.
And the heavens were completed and the earth and all its components (were completed). And God completed on the seventh day the work which God had been doing; and rested on the seventh day from all the work which had been done. And God blessed the seventh day and sanctified it, because on it, God rested from all the work which God had created through doing.

Borei p'ri ha-gafen

בָּרוּךְ אַתָּה יְיָ	*Barukh attah Adonai*
אֱלֹהֵינוּ מֶלֶךְ הָעוֹלָם	*Eloheinu melekh ha-olam*
בּוֹרֵא פְּרִי הַגָּפֶן.	*borei p'ri ha-gafen.*

Praised are You, Adonai, our God, Ruler of the universe,
Creator of the fruit of the vine.

M'kadesh ha-Shabbat

בָּרוּךְ אַתָּה יְיָ	*Barukh attah Adonai*
אֱלֹהֵינוּ מֶלֶךְ הָעוֹלָם	*Eloheinu melekh ha-olam*
אֲשֶׁר קִדְּשָׁנוּ בְּמִצְוֹתָיו	*asher kidshanu b'mitzvotav*
וְרָצָה בָנוּ	*v'ratza vanu.*
וְשַׁבַּת קָדְשׁוֹ בְּאַהֲבָה	*V'Shabbat kodsho b'ahava*
וּבְרָצוֹן	*u-v'ratzon*
הִנְחִילָנוּ	*hinḥilanu—*
זִכָּרוֹן לְמַעֲשֵׂה בְרֵאשִׁית.	*zikaron l'ma'asei v'reishit.*
כִּי הוּא יוֹם תְּחִלָּה לְמִקְרָאֵי	*Ki hu yom t'ḥilah l'mikra'ei*
קֹדֶשׁ	*kodesh—*
זֵכֶר לִיצִיאַת מִצְרָיִם.	*zekher litziyat Mitzrayim.*
כִּי בָנוּ בָחַרְתָּ	*Ki vanu vaḥarta*
וְאוֹתָנוּ קִדַּשְׁתָּ מִכָּל-	*v'otanu kidashta mikol*
הָעַמִּים	*ha-amim;*
וְשַׁבַּת קָדְשְׁךָ בְּאַהֲבָה	*v'Shabbat kodsh'kha b'ahava*
וּבְרָצוֹן	*u-v'ratzon*
הִנְחַלְתָּנוּ.	*hinḥaltanu.*
בָּרוּךְ אַתָּה יְיָ	*Barukh attah Adonai*
מְקַדֵּשׁ הַשַּׁבָּת.	*M'kadesh ha-Shabbat.*

Praised are You, Adonai, our God, Ruler of the universe, who made us holy through the commandments and who is pleased with us. And the holy Shabbat, with love and satisfaction, God gave us as an inheritance—a remembrance of the work of Creation. For it was first among the sacred days of assembly—a remembrance of the Exodus from Egypt. For you have chosen us and You have sanctified us from (among) all the peoples; and Your holy Shabbat with love and satisfaction You gave us as an inheritance. Praised are You, Adonai, Sanctifier of the Shabbat.

6

נְטִילַת יָדַיִם *NETILAT YADAYIM*
WASHING THE HANDS

As the Rabbis did in the days of the Temple, we ritually cleanse our hands in order to sanctify the act of eating. We cover our hands with water and recite:

בָּרוּךְ אַתָּה יְיָ,	*Barukh attah Adonai*
אֱלֹהֵינוּ מֶלֶךְ הָעוֹלָם,	*Eloheinu melekh ha-olam*
אֲשֶׁר קִדְּשָׁנוּ בְּמִצְוֹתָיו,	*asher kidshanu b'mitzvotav*
וְצִוָּנוּ	*v'tzivanu*
עַל נְטִילַת יָדָיִם.	*al netilat yadayim.*

Praised are You, Adonai, our God, Ruler of the universe,
who has made us holy through the commandments
and commanded us concerning the washing of hands.

7

הַמּוֹצִיא *HA-MOTZI*
BLESSING OVER BREAD

The two special Shabbat loaves, *Ḥallot*, are uncovered, and we say:

בָּרוּךְ אַתָּה יְיָ, *Barukh attah Adonai*
אֱלֹהֵינוּ מֶלֶךְ הָעוֹלָם, *Eloheinu melekh ha-olam*
הַמּוֹצִיא לֶחֶם מִן הָאָרֶץ. *ha-motzi leḥem min ha-aretz.*

Praised are You, Adonai, our God, Ruler of the universe,
who brings forth bread from the earth.

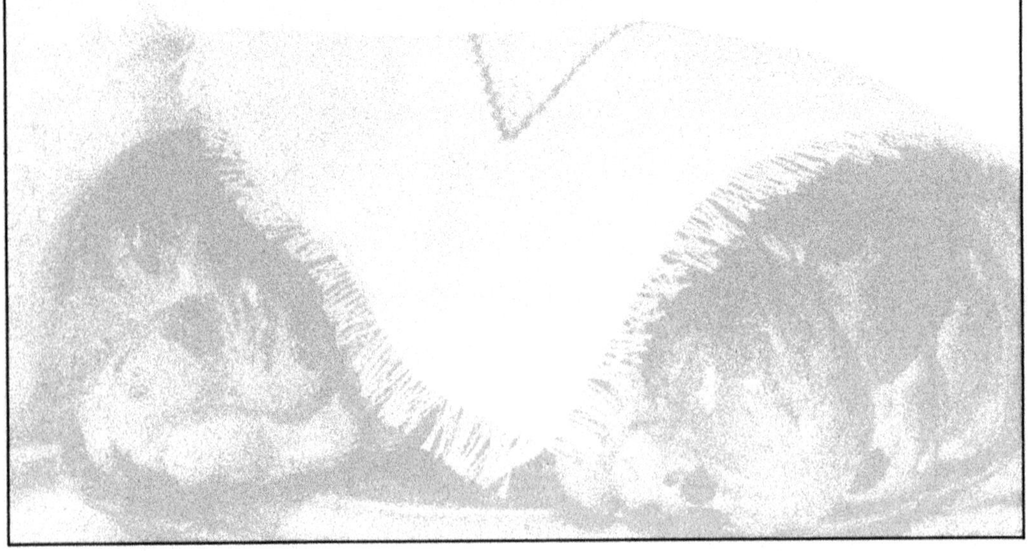

8

סְעוּדַת שַׁבָּת *SEUDAT SHABBAT*

THE SHABBAT MEAL

9

זְמִרוֹת *Z'MIROT*
SHABBAT SONGS

During our festive meal, let us share in song:

SHABBAT SHALOM

בִּים בָּם,	*Bim bam, bim bim bim bam,*
בִּים בָּם,	*Bim bim bim bim bim bam.*
שַׁבָּת שָׁלוֹם,	*Shabbat shalom,*
שַׁבָּת שָׁלוֹם	*Shabbat shalom,*
	Shabbat, Shabbat, Shabbat,
	Shabbat shalom.

L'KHAH DODI

לְכָה דוֹדִי לִקְרַאת כַּלָּה	*L'khah dodi likrat kallah*
פְּנֵי שַׁבָּת נְקַבְּלָה:	*P'nei Shabbat n'kablah.*

Come, my friend, to greet the Bride.
Let's encounter the presence of Shabbat.

שָׁמוֹר וְזָכוֹר בְּדִבּוּר אֶחָד	*Shamor v'zakhor b'dibur eḥad.*
הִשְׁמִיעָנוּ אֵל הַמְיֻחָד	*Hishmianu El ha-me'yuḥad.*
יְיָ אֶחָד וּשְׁמוֹ אֶחָד	*Adonai eḥad u-sh'mo eḥad.*
לְשֵׁם וּלְתִפְאֶרֶת וְלִתְהִלָּה:	*L'shem u-l'tiferet v'litḥilah.*
	(L'kha dodi . . .)

'Observe" and "Remember" in one word.
The One God who caused us to hear.
Adonai is One and the Divine Name is One.
To the Divine Name is the glory and the fame.

לִקְרַאת שַׁבָּת לְכוּ וְנֵלְכָה	*Likrat Shabbat l'khu v'nelkhah!*
כִּי הִיא מְקוֹר הַבְּרָכָה	*Ki hi m'kor ha-b'rakhah,*
מֵרֹאשׁ מִקֶּדֶם נְסוּכָה	*Merosh mikedem n'sukhah,*
סוֹף מַעֲשֶׂה בְּמַחֲשָׁבָה	*Sof ma'aseh b'maḥshavah*
תְּחִלָּה:	*t'ḥilah.*
	(L'kha dodi . . .)

To greet the Shabbat, let us go!
Because it is the source of blessing,
Conceived before life on earth began,
Last in God's work, first in God's thought.

הִתְעוֹרְרִי הִתְעוֹרְרִי	*Hit'or'ri hit'or'ri,*
כִּי בָא אוֹרֵךְ קוּמִי אוֹרִי	*Ki vo orekh kumi ori.*
עוּרִי עוּרִי שִׁיר דַּבֵּרִי	*Uri uri shir daberi;*
כְּבוֹד יְיָ עָלַיִךְ נִגְלָה:	*K'vod Adonai ala'yikh niglah.*
	(L'kha dodi . . .)

Arise, arise, for your light has risen,
For the dawn has broken, the light has come.
Awake, awake, and joyously sing;
The honor of Adonai is upon you and revealed.

יָמִין וּשְׂמֹאל תִּפְרוֹצִי	*Yamin u-s'mol tifrotzi;*
וְאֶת־יְיָ תַּעֲרִיצִי	*V'et Adonai ta'aritzi.*
עַל־יַד אִישׁ בֶּן־פַּרְצִי	*Al yad ish ben Partzi,*
וְנִשְׂמְחָה וְנָגִילָה:	*V'nis'm'ḥa v'nagilah.*
	(L'kha dodi . . .)

From the right to the left, you will prosper;
And you will always revere Adonai.
Through the person descended from Peretz (King David),
We will rejoice and exult.

בּוֹאִי בְשָׁלוֹם עֲטֶרֶת בַּעְלָהּ	*Bo'i v'shalom ateret balah,*
גַּם בְּשִׂמְחָה וּבְצָהֳלָה	*Gam b'simḥah u-v'tzahalah.*
תּוֹךְ אֱמוּנֵי עַם סְגֻלָּה	*Tokh emunei am s'gulah,*
בּוֹאִי כַלָּה בּוֹאִי כַלָּה:	*Bo'i khallah; bo'i khallah!*
	(L'kha dodi . . .)

Come in peace, crown of her husband,
Come in happiness and with good cheer.
Amidst the faithful of the treasured people,
Come, Bride; Come, Bride!

YISM'ḤU B'MALAKHUT'KHA

יִשְׂמְחוּ בְּמַלְכוּתְךָ	*Yism'ḥu b'malakhut'kha*
שׁוֹמְרֵי	*Shomrei, shomrei, shomrei*
שַׁבָּת	*Shabbat,*
וְקוֹרְאֵי עֹנֶג שַׁבָּת.	*v'korei oneg Shabbat.*

Rejoice in Your reign, Observe the Shabbat. Call the Shabbat a delight.

ELEH ḤAMDAH LIBI

אֵלֶּה חָמְדָה לִבִּי	*Eleh ḥamda libi*
חוּסָה נָּא וְאַל נָא תִּתְעַלֵּם.	*Ḥusa na v'al na titalem.*

Be merciful, my beloved, and pray, do not hide from us.

TZUR MISHELO

צוּר מִשֶּׁלּוֹ אָכַלְנוּ	*Tzur mishelo akhalnu*
בָּרְכוּ אֱמוּנַי	*Bar'khu emunai*
שָׂבַעְנוּ וְהוֹתַרְנוּ	*Savanu v'hotarnu*
כִּדְבַר יְיָ:	*Kid'var Adonai.*

Our Rock, from whose goodness we have eaten,
Let us praise our God, my faithful ones.
We have satisfied ourselves and we have left over (food)
According to the word of Adonai.

הַזָּן אֶת־עוֹלָמוֹ	*Hazan et olamo*
רוֹעֵנוּ אָבִינוּ	*Ro'einu avinu*
אָכַלְנוּ אֶת־לַחְמוֹ	*Akhalnu et laḥmo*
וְיֵינוֹ שָׁתִינוּ	*V'yeino shatinu.*
עַל־כֵּן נוֹדֶה לִשְׁמוֹ	*Al ken nodeh lishmo*
וּנְהַלְלוֹ בְּפִינוּ	*U-n'hal'lo b'finu.*
אָמַרְנוּ וְעָנִינוּ	*Amarnu v'aninu;*
אֵין קָדוֹשׁ כַּיְיָ:	*Ein kadosh kA'donai.*
	(*Tzur mishelo . . .*)

You feed the world,
Our Shepherd, Our Parent.
We eat of God's bread,
Of Your wine we drink.
For this, we give thanks to God
And praise God with our mouths.
We say and we answer:
None is as holy as Adonai.

בְּשִׁיר וְקוֹל תּוֹדָה	*B'shir v'kol todah*
נְבָרֵךְ אֱלֹהֵינוּ	*N'varekh le'loheinu.*
עַל־אֶרֶץ חֶמְדָּה	*Al eretz ḥemdah*
שֶׁהִנְחִיל לַאֲבוֹתֵינוּ	*She'hinḥil la'avoteinu.*
מָזוֹן וְצֵידָה	*Mazon v'tzeidah*
הִשְׂבִּיעַ לְנַפְשֵׁנוּ	*Hishbi'a l'nafsheinu.*
חַסְדּוֹ גָּבַר עָלֵינוּ	*Ḥasdo gavar aleinu*
וֶאֱמֶת יְיָ:	*V'emet Adonai.*
	(*Tzur mishelo . . .*)

With song and a voice of thanks,
We praise Our God,
For the spacious land,
Which is the inheritance of our ancestors.
Food and sustenance is rich reward to our souls.
God's gracious love determines all,
And the truth of Adonai.

HINEI MAH TOV

הִנֵּה מַה־טּוֹב וּמַה־נָּעִים	*Hinei mah tov u-mah na'im*
שֶׁבֶת אַחִים גַּם יָחַד.	*shevet aḥim gam yaḥad.*

Behold, how good and pleasant it is for brethren
to dwell together in unity.

DAVID MELEKH YISRAEL

דָּוִד מֶלֶךְ יִשְׂרָאֵל	*David, Melekh Yisrael,*
חַי וְקַיָּם.	*Ḥai, ḥai, v'kayom!*

David, King of Israel, lives forever!

LO YISA GOY

לֹא יִשָּׂא גּוֹי אֶל גּוֹי חֶרֶב	*Lo yisa goy el goy ḥerev,*
לֹא יִלְמְדוּ עוֹד מִלְחָמָה.	*Lo yilm'du od milḥamah.*

Nation shall not lift up sword against nation,
Neither shall they learn war anymore.

שִׁיר הַמַּעֲלוֹת
בְּשׁוּב יְיָ אֶת־שִׁיבַת
צִיּוֹן
הָיִינוּ כְּחֹלְמִים:
אָז יִמָּלֵא
שְׂחוֹק פִּינוּ
וּלְשׁוֹנֵנוּ
רִנָּה.
אָז יֹאמְרוּ בַגּוֹיִם
הִגְדִּיל יְיָ לַעֲשׂוֹת עִם־
אֵלֶּה:
הִגְדִּיל יְיָ לַעֲשׂוֹת עִמָּנוּ,
הָיִינוּ שְׂמֵחִים:
שׁוּבָה יְיָ אֶת־שְׁבִיתֵנוּ
כַּאֲפִיקִים בַּנֶּגֶב:
הַזֹּרְעִים בְּדִמְעָה,
בְּרִנָּה יִקְצֹרוּ:
הָלוֹךְ יֵלֵךְ וּבָכֹה,
נֹשֵׂא מֶשֶׁךְ־הַזָּרַע.
בֹּא־יָבֹא בְרִנָּה,
נֹשֵׂא אֲלֻמֹּתָיו:

10

בִּרְכַּת הַמָּזוֹן *BIRKAT HA-MAZON*
BLESSING AFTER FOOD

To complete our Shabbat Seder, we praise God for providing us good food, our families and friends, and the Shabbat itself:

SHIR HA-MA'ALOT

Shir ha-Ma'alot:	A song of ascents:
B'shuv Adonai et shivat Tzion	When Adonai restores the fortunes of Zion,
hayinu k'ḥolmim.	we will be as in a dream.
Az yimalei s'ḥok pinu	Then our mouths will be filled with laughter
u-l'shoneinu rina.	and our tongues (filled with) songs of joy.
Az yomru va'goyim:	Then they will say among the nations:
"Higdil Adonai la'asot im eileh."	"Adonai did great things for them."
Higdil Adonai la'asot imanu;	Adonai will do great things for us;
hayinu s'meiḥim.	we will be happy.
Shuva Adonai et sh'viteinu	The Lord will restore our fortune
ka'afikim ba'Negev.	like streams in the Negev.
Ha-zorim b'dima	Those who sow in tears,
b'rina yiktzoru;	with songs they shall reap;
Halokh yeilekh u-vakho	One who walks along and weeps,
nosei meshekh ha-zara—	carrying a sack of seeds—
boyavo v'rina,	that one will come back with song,
nosei alumotav.	carrying sheaves.

חַבֵרַי נְבָרֵךְ:

יְהִי שֵׁם יְיָ
מְבֹרָךְ מֵעַתָּה וְעַד עוֹלָם:

יְהִי שֵׁם יְיָ מְבֹרָךְ
מֵעַתָּה וְעַד עוֹלָם:
בִּרְשׁוּת חַבֵרַי
נְבָרֵךְ (אֱלֹהֵינוּ)
שֶׁאָכַלְנוּ מִשֶּׁלּוֹ:

בָּרוּךְ (אֱלֹהֵינוּ)
שֶׁאָכַלְנוּ מִשֶּׁלּוֹ:
וּבְטוּבוֹ חָיִינוּ:

בָּרוּךְ (אֱלֹהֵינוּ)
שֶׁאָכַלְנוּ מִשֶּׁלּוֹ
וּבְטוּבוֹ חָיִינוּ:

בָּרוּךְ הוּא וּבָרוּךְ שְׁמוֹ:

ZIMMUN

The *Zimmun* is recited responsively when there are 3 or more adults present. The word *Eloheinu* is added to the *Zimmun* if 10 or more adults are present.

Leader

Ḥaverai n'varekh.	My friends, let us praise.

Everyone

Yehi shem Adonai	May Adonai's name be praised from
m'vorakh me'attah v'ad olam.	now and until forever.

Leader

Yehi shem Adonai m'vorakh	May Adonai's name be praised
me'attah v'ad olam.	from now and until forever.
Bir'shut ḥaverai,	With the consent of my friends,
nevarekh (Eloheinu)	let us praise (our God) the One whose
she'akhalnu mishelo.	food we have eaten.

Everyone

Barukh (Eloheinu)	Praised is (our God) the One of whose
she'akhalnu mishelo	(food) we have eaten,
u-v'tuvo ḥayinu.	and by whose goodness we live.

Leader

Barukh (Eloheinu)	Praised is (our God) the One of whose
she'akhalnu mishelo	(food) we have eaten,
u-v'tuvo ḥayinu.	and by whose goodness we live.

Everyone

Barukh hu u-varukh sh'mo.	Praised be God and praised be God's name.

בָּרוּךְ אַתָּה יְהוָֹה
אֱלֹהֵינוּ מֶלֶךְ הָעוֹלָם
הַזָּן אֶת־הָעוֹלָם
כֻּלּוֹ בְּטוּבוֹ
בְּחֵן בְּחֶסֶד וּבְרַחֲמִים

הוּא נוֹתֵן לֶחֶם לְכָל־בָּשָׂר
כִּי לְעוֹלָם חַסְדּוֹ
וּבְטוּבוֹ הַגָּדוֹל תָּמִיד לֹא
חָסַר לָנוּ
וְאַל יֶחְסַר לָנוּ מָזוֹן לְעוֹלָם
וָעֶד
בַּעֲבוּר שְׁמוֹ הַגָּדוֹל
כִּי הוּא אֵל זָן וּמְפַרְנֵס לַכֹּל

וּמֵטִיב לַכֹּל
וּמֵכִין מָזוֹן לְכָל־
בְּרִיּוֹתָיו
אֲשֶׁר בָּרָא:
בָּרוּךְ אַתָּה יְהוָֹה הַזָּן
אֶת־הַכֹּל:

HAZAN ET HA-KOL

Barukh attah Adonai	Praised are You, Adonai,
Eloheinu melekh ha-olam	Our God, Ruler of the universe,
hazan et ha-olam	who feeds the world,
kulo b'tuvo	all of it with goodness,
b'ḥen b'ḥesed u-v'raḥamim.	with graciousness, with love, and with compassion.
Hu notein leḥem l'khol basar	God provides food to every creature
ki l'olam ḥasdo.	because Divine love (endures) forever.
U-v'tuvo ha-gadol tamid lo	And through it, God's great goodness
ḥasar lanu	has never failed us,
v'al yeḥ'sar lanu mazon l'olam va'ed	and food will not fail us ever,
ba'avur sh'mo ha-gadol.	for the sake of God's great name.
Ki hu El zan u-m'farnes la-kol	Because God who feeds provides for all,
u-meitiv la-kol	and does good for all,
u-mei'khin mazon l'khol b'riyotav	and prepares food for all creatures
asher bara.	which God created.
Barukh attah Adonai Hazan	Praised are You Adonai,
et ha-kol.	the Provider of food for all.

נוֹדֶה לְךָ יְיָ אֱלֹהֵינוּ
עַל שֶׁהִנְחַלְתָּ לַאֲבוֹתֵינוּ
אֶרֶץ חֶמְדָּה טוֹבָה וּרְחָבָה,
בְּרִית וְתוֹרָה, חַיִּים וּמָזוֹן.

יִתְבָּרַךְ שִׁמְךָ
בְּפִי כָּל־חַי תָּמִיד לְעוֹלָם
וָעֶד,
כַּכָּתוּב:
וְאָכַלְתָּ וְשָׂבָעְתָּ

וּבֵרַכְתָּ אֶת־יְיָ
אֱלֹהֶיךָ
עַל הָאָרֶץ הַטּוֹבָה אֲשֶׁר
נָתַן לָךְ.
בָּרוּךְ אַתָּה יְיָ,
עַל הָאָרֶץ וְעַל הַמָּזוֹן.

וּבְנֵה יְרוּשָׁלַיִם
עִיר הַקֹּדֶשׁ בִּמְהֵרָה
בְיָמֵינוּ
בָּרוּךְ אַתָּה יְיָ
בּוֹנֶה בְרַחֲמָיו
יְרוּשָׁלָיִם. אָמֵן.

AL HA-ARETZ V'AL HA-MAZON

Nodeh lekha Adonai Eloheinu	We thank You Adonai, Our God,
al she'binḥalta la'avoteinu:	for Your inheritance to our ancestors:
eretz ḥemdah tovah u-r'ḥavah	a land—desirable, good, and spacious,
b'rit v'Torah ḥayim u-mazon.	the covenant and the Torah, life and food.
Yitbarakh shimkha	May Your name be praised
b'fi khol ḥai tamid l'olam va'ed.	by the mouth of every living thing.
Kakatuv:	As it is written:
"v'akhalta v'savata	"and (when) you have eaten, and are satisfied,
u-veirakhta et Adonai Elohekha	you shall praise Adonai, Your God,
al ha-aretz ha-tovah asher natan lakh."	for the good land which He gave to you."
Barukh attah Adonai	Praised are You, Adonai,
al ha-aretz ve'al ha-mazon.	for the land and for the sustenance.

BIRKAT YERUSHALAYIM

U-v'nei Yerushalayim	Rebuild Jerusalem,
ir ha-kodesh bim'heirah v'yameinu.	the Holy City, soon, and in our days.
Barukh attah Adonai	Praised are You, Adonai,
boneh v'raḥamav	who with compassion rebuilds
Yerushalayim, Amen.	Jerusalem, Amen.

בָּרוּךְ אַתָּה יְיָ,
אֱלֹהֵינוּ מֶלֶךְ הָעוֹלָם,
הַמֶּלֶךְ הַטּוֹב וְהַמֵּטִיב
לַכֹּל.
הוּא הֵטִיב, הוּא מֵטִיב.
הוּא יֵטִיב לָנוּ.
הוּא גְמָלָנוּ הוּא גוֹמְלֵנוּ

הוּא יִגְמְלֵנוּ לָעַד
חֵן וָחֶסֶד וְרַחֲמִים
וִיזַכֵּנוּ לִימוֹת הַמָּשִׁיחַ.

הָרַחֲמָן הוּא יַנְחִילֵנוּ

יוֹם שֶׁכֻּלּוֹ שַׁבָּת
וּמְנוּחָה לְחַיֵּי הָעוֹלָמִים.

BIRKAT HA-TOVAH

Barukh attah Adonai	Praised are You, Adonai,
Eloheinu melekh ha-olam	Our God, Ruler of the universe,
ha-melekh ha-tov v'ha-meitiv	the Ruler who is good and does good
la-kol.	for all.
Hu heitiv hu meitiv	God has been good, God is good,
hu yeitiv lanu.	God will be good to us.
Hu gemalanu hu gomleinu	God bestowed upon us, God bestows upon us,
hu yigm'leinu la'ad	God will bestow upon us forever,
ḥen vaḥesed veraḥamim	grace, kindness, and compassion,
vizakeinu limot ha-mashiaḥ.	and gain for us the days of the Messiah.

HA-RAḤAMAN

Ha-Raḥaman hu yanḥileinu	(May) the Merciful One give us as an inheritance
yom she'kulo Shabbat	a day that is completely Shabbat,
u-menuḥa l'ḥayei ha-olamim.	and rest in life everlasting in the world to come.

וְנִשָּׂא בְרָכָה מֵאֵת
יְיָ
וּצְדָקָה מֵאֱלֹהֵי
יִשְׁעֵנוּ
וְנִמְצָא חֵן
וְשֵׂכֶל טוֹב
בְּעֵינֵי אֱלֹהִים וְאָדָם.
עֹשֶׂה שָׁלוֹם בִּמְרוֹמָיו

הוּא יַעֲשֶׂה שָׁלוֹם עָלֵינוּ
וְעַל כָּל-יִשְׂרָאֵל, וְאִמְרוּ אָמֵן.

OSEH SHALOM

Venisa verakha mei'eit	Then shall we receive blessing from
Adonai	Adonai
u-tzedakah me'Elohei	and justice from the God of our
yisheinu.	deliverance.
Venimtza ḥen	And may we find favor and good
veseikhel tov	understanding
b'einei Elohim v'adam.	in the eyes of God and people.
Oseh shalom	The One who makes peace in the
bimromov	heavens,
hu ya'aseh shalom aleinu	(May) that One make peace for us
v'al kol Yisrael v'imru, Amen.	and for all Israel, and let us say, Amen.

About the Federation of Jewish Men's Clubs

The Federation of Jewish Men's Clubs (FJMC) is the male volunteer arm of the Conservative/Masorti Movement. Created in 1929 to "involve men in Jewish life," the FJMC enriches the quality of Jewish life and creates ways of instilling passion and enthusiasm through its numerous programmatic initiatives. The FJMC promotes Conservative/Masorti Judaism worldwide through the World Wide Wrap (worldwidewrap.org), the Shoah Yellow Candles observance, and the Outreach to Intermarrieds (Keruv) initiative. Most recent efforts focus on attracting and engaging men more actively as volunteers in their local communities.

For a complete list of publications, films, and services, visit their website at www.fjmc.org.

About JEWISH LIGHTS Publishing

People of all faiths and backgrounds yearn for books that attract, engage, educate, and spiritually inspire.

Our principal goal is to stimulate thought and help all people learn about who the Jewish People are, where they come from, and what the future can be made to hold. While people of our diverse Jewish heritage are the primary audience, our books speak to people in the Christian world as well and will broaden their understanding of Judaism and the roots of their own faith.

We bring to you authors who are at the forefront of spiritual thought and experience. While each has something different to say, they all say it in a voice that you can hear.

Our books are designed to welcome you and then to engage, stimulate, and inspire. We judge our success not only by whether or not our books are beautiful and commercially successful, but by whether or not they make a difference in your life.

We at Jewish Lights take great care to produce beautiful books that present meaningful spiritual content in a form that reflects the art of making high-quality books.

Also by Dr. Ron Wolfson to Enrich Your Shabbat Experience

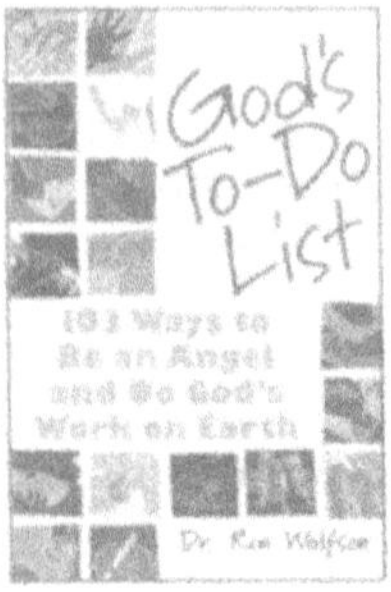

God's To-Do List

103 Ways to Be an Angel and Do God's Work on Earth

This practical guidebook to repairing the world—often in simple, everyday ways—details the biblical accounts of what God does, not what God says: God creates, blesses, rests, calls, comforts, cares, repairs, wrestles, gives and forgives. This provocative resource suggests what might be on God's To-Do List for you.

6 x 9, 144 pp, Quality Paperback Original
ISBN 978-1-58023-301-9

The Spirituality of Welcoming

How to Transform Your Congregation into a Sacred Community

This empowering, practical guide explores how to transform your synagogue or organization into a sacred community by creating a culture founded on the spirituality of welcome.

6 x 9, 224 pp, Quality Paperback Original
ISBN 978-1-58023-244-9

Manufactured in the United States of America

Published by Jewish Lights Publishing

www.jewishlights.com